DRY
JANUARY

DRY

JANUARY

**101 ALCOHOL-FREE TIPS
TO GET YOU TO FEBRUARY**

STEPHANIE GLASS

PORTICO

CONTENTS

WELCOME TO DRY JANUARY!

As a writer myself and, like most of my profession, a purely social drinker, I was quite shocked to discover that anyone would ever *need* tips on getting through a month without alcohol – surely it's easy! I was discussing it once with a fellow hack and he said, 'Stephanie, quite frankly, it's a piece of cake... as long as I can find enough pieces of cake to eat, I don't have time to drink.'

But then I was dared to tackle Dry January myself last year and I must admit found it harder than I'd anticipated. I wouldn't have completed it at all had it not been for the odd little cheat I allowed myself – wine with a meal is obviously food, which doesn't count; a nightcap is more or less medicine if you have my bedtime problems – but it was pedantically drawn to my attention that, apparently, this was against the spirit of the whole thing. So, I decided what I needed if I was going to do it properly was a helping hand, a guidebook of useful tips to encourage me when the going got tough and, just occasionally, the well-meaning crack of a whip and smack of firm government to keep me on the straight and narrow.

Well, reader, I was astonished to discover that such a book does not exist. There are volumes devoted to helping you give up the demon drink altogether, and I'm sure they're jolly useful for people who want or need to do that. But they all seem

First published in the United Kingdom
in 2016 by
Portico
1 Gower Street
London
WC1E 6HD

An imprint of Pavilion Books Company Ltd

ISBN 978-1-91104-253-2

A CIP catalogue record for this book is available
from the British Library.

10 9 8 7 6 5 4 3 2 1

Reproduction by Mission Productions Ltd, Hong Kong

Printed and bound by 1010 Printing International Ltd, China

This book can be ordered direct from the publisher at
www.pavilionbooks.com

– understandably – a little bit . . . worthy. I mean, lectures in quantum physics are probably fascinating to those who want to devote a lifetime to cracking the mysteries of the Universe, but the rest of us who only want to get next month's science GCSE out of the way as painlessly as possible would rather just have a few snappy mnemonics to remember Boyle's Law and the colours of the rainbow.

So, for my own sake, and for anyone else who just wants to dip a toe into the murky waters of abstemiousness, I decided to write a guide to Dry January that was bite-sized, comprehensible, and not entirely serious. After all, it's going to be a tough month, so we'll all need cheering up. One thing you'll need to decide is: 'When does Dry January start? Can I have a drink after Big Ben on New Year's Eve?' Well, it very much depends how big Ben is and whether you can pinch his drink without him noticing. My stance is that if you have a few drinks in the small hours of New Year's Day, then you can't justify waiting up until midnight on 31 January and immediately start gratefully necking down the Pinot Grigio. Consistency is the key.

The tips at the beginning of this book will be focused on handy preparations to make for the month ahead, while those later on are aimed at getting you over the tricky finishing line at the end. In between is a wealth of ideas to keep you off the booze for 31 days straight, including advice on how to cope with 'trigger points': weddings, christenings, funerals . . . anything involving having a good time, basically.

So throw out your bottle opener, get reading, and I'll see you on 1 February . . .

①

BUY
THIS
BOOK!

(2)

BUY A TEAR-OFF DESK CALENDAR AND IMMEDIATELY REMOVE THE FIRST 30 DAYS – LOOK AT IT WHEN YOU WAKE UP AND KID YOURSELF THERE'S ONLY ONE DAY TO GO! (ALTERNATIVELY, IF YOU LIKE THE IDEA OF TEARING OFF JANUARY 30 EACH MORNING TO JOYOUSLY REVEAL THE FINAL DAY, JUST BUY 31 DESK CALENDARS INSTEAD AND SET THEM ALL TO 30 JANUARY.)

CELEBRATE NEW YEAR'S EVE AT HOME: INVITE EVERYONE YOU KNOW TO A 'DON'T BRING A BOTTLE PARTY', THEN CHALLENGE THEM TO EMPTY YOUR DRINKS CABINET BY THE END OF THE NIGHT. A GIANT PUNCHBOWL WILL COME IN HANDY TO FINISH OFF THE DREGS.

4

GIVE A PERSONAL BREATHALYSER
MACHINE TO YOUR BEST FRIEND
FOR CHRISTMAS AND TELL THEM
THEY CAN CALL AT YOUR HOUSE
UNANNOUNCED AT ANY TIME
THROUGHOUT JANUARY WITH IT.
PROMISE TO GIVE THEM £500 IF
THEY BREATHALYSE YOU AND FIND
ALCOHOL IN YOUR SYSTEM. YOU
CAN EXPECT TO SEE A GREAT DEAL
OF YOUR FRIEND THIS MONTH!

⑤

GO ON FACEBOOK

ON NEW YEAR'S EVE AND UNFRIEND ANYONE WITH A

BIRTHDAY IN JANUARY.

6

HAVE TWO JARS IN YOUR
HOUSE – EVERY EVENING
THAT YOU WOULD HAVE GONE
TO THE PUB, STICK A FIVER
IN EACH JAR. AT THE END OF
THE MONTH USE ONE JAR TO
TREAT YOURSELF AND GIVE
THE OTHER TO A FAVOURITE
GOOD CAUSE.

7

IF YOU ARE A COUPLE
PLANNING ON STARTING
A FAMILY, GET BUSY ABOUT
NOVEMBER – THAT WAY,
COME THE END OF THE YEAR,
YOU MAY HAVE THE PERFECT
EXCUSE TO GIVE UP THE BOOZE.
SUPPORTIVE FATHERS-TO-BE WILL
JOIN THEIR PARTNERS IN RESISTING
A BEVVY – TILL 1 FEBRUARY AT THE
VERY LEAST! OR IF YOU'RE A GAL
WITH NO PLANS TO CONCEIVE,
WHY NOT JUST *TELL* EVERYONE
YOU'RE PREGNANT – THEY'LL BE
FALLING OVER THEMSELVES TO
STOP YOU HAVING A TIPPLE!

8

PUT A LOCK ON YOUR DRINKS CABINET AND GIVE A FRIEND THE KEY. JUST MAKE SURE IT'S NOT THE SAME FRIEND YOU GAVE THE PERSONAL BREATHALYSER MACHINE TO (SEE TIP 4)!

9

GET SO SLOSHED ON
NEW YEAR'S EVE
THAT YOU CAN'T FACE A
DRINK
FOR AT LEAST
A WEEK.

IF YOU LOOK UNDER 25
(I HATE YOU, BY THE WAY),
BURN ALL YOUR FORMS OF
ID BEFORE JANUARY STARTS.
REAPPLYING FOR ALL THESE
VITAL DOCUMENTS WILL
ALSO GIVE YOU PLENTY TO
DO IN JANUARY TO TAKE
YOUR MIND OFF ALCOHOL.

**TELL EVERYONE YOU KNOW
THAT YOU'RE GOING DRY –
IF THEY'RE REAL FRIENDS
THEY'LL ENCOURAGE YOU.**

12

PUT A
JUICER
ON YOUR
CHRISTMAS LIST.

PRACTICAL

(13)

WHEN SENDING OUT
YOUR CHRISTMAS CARDS,
POP IN AN INVITE TO A
PARTY AT YOURS FOR
1 FEBRUARY TO CELEBRATE
THE END OF DRY JANUARY –
NOW YOU'VE GOT SOMETHING
TO LOOK FORWARD TO.

BONUS TIP KEEP YOURSELF
BUSY IN JANUARY MAKING
BUNTING FOR YOUR POST-DROUGHT
KNEES-UP – SOMETHING TO DO
DURING THOSE LONG EVENINGS
NOT SPENT AT THE PUB.

14

BUY A BOOK OF MOCKTAIL RECIPES AND GET MIXING.

15

GET A JOB ON AN OIL RIG FOR A
MONTH. THERE'S A STRICTLY NO
ALCOHOL/NO SMOKING POLICY
OFFSHORE, SO IT'S A GREAT WAY
TO KICK THE NICOTINE HABIT TOO.

DESPERATE

MEASURES

16

GET PEOPLE TO SPONSOR
YOU TO GIVE UP FOR A
GOOD CAUSE DEAR TO YOUR
HEART – IT WILL GIVE YOU
EXTRA MOTIVATION.

SIGN UP
FOR A MONTH-LONG,
CLINIC-BASED
MEDICAL
TRIAL.

18

PERSUADE THE REST OF YOUR HOUSE TO JOIN IN DRY JANUARY — IT'S MUCH EASIER WHEN YOU'RE DOING IT TOGETHER, PLUS THEY WON'T BE DRINKING IN FRONT OF YOU AND TEMPTING YOU.

19

IF THERE'S AN UNREPENTANT
TIPPLER IN YOUR HOUSE,
DESIGNATE ONE ROOM AS
ALCOHOL-FREE FOR THE MONTH
– THEN YOU'LL ALWAYS HAVE A
BOLT-HOLE IF THE SIGHT OF
THAT OPEN BOTTLE OF COLD
LAGER IS TOO MUCH.

IF YOU HAVE A FAVOURITE
WATERING HOLE, DO SOMETHING
UNSPEAKABLE THERE ON NEW
YEAR'S EVE TO GET YOURSELF
BARRED. IF THEY REFUSE TO BAR
YOU, ASK THEM NOT TO SERVE
YOU ALCOHOL DURING JANUARY,
HOWEVER MUCH YOU PLEAD –
PROMISE TO DRINK TWICE AS MUCH
IN FEBRUARY TO MAKE UP FOR IT.

21

THROW AWAY ALL YOUR BOTTLE
OPENERS, EVEN THE NOVELTY
FARTING ONE – YOU CAN ALWAYS
BUY ANOTHER ONE IN FEBRUARY.

22

AS A NEW YEAR'S RESOLUTION, BECOME A BUDDHIST.

23

IF YOU'D NORMALLY HAVE A
DRINK FOR 'DUTCH COURAGE',
REMEMBER THE WORDS OF
ROSS MACDONALD:

**"POUR ALCOHOL
ON A BUNDLE
OF NERVES AND
IT GENERALLY
TURNS INTO A
CAN OF WORMS."**

24

IF THE THOUGHT OF GOING
COLD TURKEY STRAIGHT AFTER
CHRISTMAS IS JUST TOO HARD
TO CONTEMPLATE, CONSIDER
DOING DRY FEBRUARY INSTEAD.
IT'S GOT THREE FEWER DAYS –
AS LONG AS IT ISN'T A LEAP YEAR!

25

MAKE YOUR OWN DRY JANUARY
PLAYLIST. HERE ARE THREE
TO GET YOU STARTED.

'BAD, BAD WHISKEY'
(AMOS MILBURN)

'SOBER'
(PINK)

'THE BOTTLE LET ME DOWN'
(MERLE HAGGARD)

(26)

**IF YOU'RE MEETING FRIENDS,
SUGGEST GOING TO COFFEE BARS
INSTEAD OF PUBS.**

(27)

DO YOUR GROCERY
SHOPPING ONLINE SO
YOU DON'T HAVE TO
WALK PAST ROWS OF
CUT-PRICE PLONK IN
THE SUPERMARKET.

(28)

THERE ARE *LOADS* OF ALCOHOL-FREE BEERS AND WINES OUT THERE NOWADAYS – IT'S NOT ALL EISBERG AND ST CHRISTOPHER – YOU CAN EVEN BUY 0% SPIRITS! THERE ARE MORE THAN ENOUGH TO TRY A DIFFERENT ONE EVERY NIGHT, AND IF BY THE END OF THE MONTH ALL YOU'VE DECIDED IS THAT YOU DON'T LIKE ANY OF THEM, CHEER UP – IT'S FEBRUARY TOMORROW.

(29)

DELIBERATELY

GET INFECTED WITH AN

ILLNESS

REQUIRING A MONTH-LONG

COURSE OF
STRONG

ANTIBIOTICS.

30

**GOOD REASONS TO DO
DRY JANUARY #1**

YOU WILL LOSE WEIGHT (AS LONG
AS YOU REPLACE THE BOOZE WITH
WATER OR LOW-CALORIE MIXERS).

31

IF THERE'S A TV PROGRAMME
THAT YOU ALWAYS SIT DOWN TO
WATCH WITH A GLASS OF WINE,
DO SOMETHING ELSE WHILE IT'S ON
AND WATCH IT ON CATCH-UP OVER
BREAKFAST THE NEXT MORNING –
JUST MAKE SURE YOU PUT MILK NOT
MERLOT ON YOUR CORNFLAKES!

32

STOP LISTENING
TO THE NEWS –
OR ANYTHING ELSE
ON TV/RADIO THAT
NORMALLY DRIVES
YOU TO DRINK.

33

IF WINE IS YOUR TIPPLE,
JUST EAT FOOD THAT
DOESN'T GO WITH
WINE. HERE ARE THREE
TO START YOU OFF:
ARTICHOKES AND
ASPARAGUS; BEANS ON
TOAST; SCRAMBLED EGGS.

34

DRINKING DOES NOT MAKE
YOU CLEVER, AS THE BARD
WAS WELL AWARE:

"**O GOD, THAT
MEN SHOULD PUT
AN ENEMY IN
THEIR MOUTHS TO
STEAL AWAY
THEIR BRAINS!**"

(*OTHELLO*, ACT II, SCENE III)

35

ABSTINENCE MAKES THE
HEART GROW FONDER:
FALL IN LOVE WITH YOUR
PARTNER ALL OVER AGAIN
AS YOU GO OUT FOR
ALCOHOL-FREE DATES
TO THE CINEMA.

36

KEEP A DRY JANUARY DIARY,
NOTING DIFFICULT TIMES OF DAY,
TRIGGER POINTS, ETC. AND HOW
YOU COPED WITH THEM.

PRACTICAL

37

PUT ENCOURAGING POST-IT NOTES AROUND THE HOUSE.

YOU CAN
DO IT!

ONE
WEEK
ALREADY!

YOU'RE
FEELING
SO MUCH
BETTER!

38

IF YOU WANT SOMETHING TO PUT
YOU OFF THE HARD STUFF FOR
GOOD, NEVER MIND JANUARY,
TRY SEARCHING THESE TERMS ON
YOUTUBE: 'DRUNK PEOPLE DOING
STUPID THINGS'; 'DRUNK PEOPLE
STAIRS'; 'DRUNK PEOPLE DANCING'.

39

LOOK OUT FOR WITHDRAWAL
SYMPTOMS AND BE READY
FOR THEM. TYPICAL ONES
INCLUDE HEADACHES CAUSED
BY DEHYDRATION (SOLUTION:
PAINKILLERS AND DRINK PLENTY
OF WATER) AND SUGAR CRAVING
(SOLUTION: GIVE IN TO IT
– THOSE CHRISTMAS CHOCS
WON'T EAT THEMSELVES).

40

ACUPUNCTURE
CAN BE TARGETED TO HELP YOU
GIVE UP
THINGS LIKE BOOZE
AND CIGGIES, SO WHY NOT
GIVE IT A TRY.
IF NOTHING ELSE, IT'S HARMLESS
AND RELAXING, AND THE
MONEY YOU'VE SAVED
ON ALCOHOL WILL EASILY
PAY FOR A SESSION.

(41)

TRIGGER POINTS #1
WEDDINGS

MANY PEOPLE MEET THEIR NEXT
PARTNER AT WEDDING RECEPTIONS,
AND LOOK HOW MOST OF THEM
TURN OUT. THE MAJORITY OF THESE
RELATIONSHIPS WILL START UNDER
THE INFLUENCE. AVOID THE RISK
AND STAY SOBER.

(42)

GET A FRIENDLY HYPNOTIST
TO CONVINCE YOU THAT YOUR
FAVOURITE TIPPLE TASTES LIKE
WASHING-UP LIQUID.

(43)

ERNEST HEMINGWAY SAID,

"ALWAYS DO SOBER WHAT YOU SAID YOU'D DO DRUNK."

YOU'D THINK THIS WAS GOOD ADVICE THAT WOULD LEAD YOU NOT TO DRINK, BUT IN FACT HE CONCLUDED,

"THAT WILL TEACH YOU TO KEEP YOUR MOUTH SHUT!"

REMEMBER, ALCOHOL NOT
ONLY MAKES YOU FAT,
IT ALSO MAKES YOU LEAN
. . . USUALLY OVER THE
TOILET BOWL.

45

IF YOU'RE REALLY STRUGGLING, WHY NOT POP DOWN TO YOUR LOCAL MAGISTRATES' COURT AND START BEING RUDE TO THE JP – KEEP GOING UNTIL THE SENTENCE REACHES THE NUMBER OF DAYS LEFT IN JANUARY, THEN POLITELY SAY, 'THANK YOU, YOUR HONOUR,' AND PUT YOUR HANDS OUT FOR THE CUFFS.

BONUS TIP DON'T FORGET TO BEHAVE BADLY ENOUGH IN THE CLINK SO YOU WON'T BE LET OUT EARLY.

(46)

AS DOCTOR WHO, ARTHUR DENT, C.S. LEWIS AND WEDGIE BENN CAN ALL ATTEST, THERE IS ABSOLUTELY NOTHING IN THIS WORLD LIKE A NICE CUP OF TEA. WITH OVER 3,000 VARIETIES OUT THERE, EVEN IF YOU'RE AN ARDENT TEA-NOT-AT-ALL-ER, THERE MUST BE ONE FOR YOU.

IN MY BOOK – AND, LET'S FACE IT,
THIS *IS* MY BOOK – FOOD ISN'T
ALCOHOL, SO HERE'S A CHEAT'S TIP:

TREAT YOURSELF TO COQ-AU-VIN
OR BEER-BATTERED FISH, POLISHED
OFF WITH SHERRY TRIFLE.

DON'T WHINGE ABOUT YOUR WORK WHILE GOING DRY, OR SOMEONE IS LIKELY TO QUOTE DREW CAREY AT YOU:

"OH, YOU HATE YOUR JOB? THERE'S A SUPPORT GROUP FOR THAT. IT'S CALLED

EVERYBODY

AND THEY MEET AT THE BAR."

49

IF IT'S YOUR BIRTHDAY IN
JANUARY YOU HAVE A CHOICE:
POSTPONE IT UNTIL FEBRUARY,
OR HAVE A DAY OFF AND ADD IT
ON TO THE START OF FEBRUARY.
I'M NOT YOUR PRIEST, SO I
CAN'T ABSOLVE YOU IF YOU
FALL OFF THE WAGON FOR
24 HOURS . . . JUST BEAR IN MIND
IT MIGHT MAKE CLIMBING BACK
ON A BIT MORE DIFFICULT.

50

MAKE A LIST OF ALL THE
NAMES YOU CAN THINK
OF THAT MEAN DRUNK.
I'LL START YOU OFF:

HAMMERED
PLASTERED
SMASHED

ARE YOU DETECTING A
THEME HERE? IT'S NOT AN
APPEALING ONE, IS IT?

51

GOOD REASONS TO DO DRY JANUARY #2

IT'S LIKE SENDING
YOUR LIVER ON A
MONTH'S HOLIDAY –
IT WILL LOVE IT!
(JUST DON'T EXPECT
A POSTCARD!)

52

EAT OUT AT NON-LICENSED PREMISES – THERE ARE LOTS OF CURRY HOUSES IN PARTICULAR WHERE YOU HAVE TO BRING YOUR OWN BEER AND WINE IF YOU WANT IT.

(53)

LOCATE YOUR LOCAL TOWN DRUNK
AND SPEND A COUPLE OF HOURS
WATCHING HIM WEAVE HIS WAY
FROM PUB TO PUB. JUST THINK
– THAT COULD BE YOU. (THE BAD
NEWS – IF YOU CAN'T FIND YOUR
LOCAL DRUNK, IT PROBABLY *IS* YOU.)

KEEP A RUNNING TOTAL
OF ALL THE
MONEY
YOU'RE SAVING.
AND START WRITING THAT
SHOPPING LIST
OF HOW YOU PLAN TO
SPEND IT!

55

IF YOU FIND YOURSELF
STRUGGLING AT WINE
O'CLOCK EVERY NIGHT,
GO TO BED REALLY
EARLY AND RE-ADJUST
YOUR BODY CLOCK FOR
THE MONTH. YOU'LL GET
LOADS DONE EARLY THE
NEXT MORNING TOO.

56

"A COMPUTER LETS YOU MAKE MORE MISTAKES FASTER THAN ANY OTHER INVENTION, WITH THE POSSIBLE EXCEPTIONS OF HANDGUNS AND TEQUILA."

(MITCH RATCLIFFE)

57

**VOLUNTEER TO BE A
DESIGNATED DRIVER
FOR AS MANY PEOPLE
AS YOU CAN – OR SIGN
UP AS AN UBER DRIVER
FOR THE MONTH AND
GET PAID FOR IT!**

PRACTICAL

58

IF BEER IS YOUR TIPPLE
. . . JUST EAT FOOD THAT
DOESN'T GO WITH BEER.
HERE ARE THREE TO START
YOU OFF: CORNFLAKES;
MULLIGATAWNY SOUP;
KNICKERBOCKER GLORY.

59

MAKE A LIST OF THE
BEST DRY JANUARY FILMS
TO CATCH UP ON. HERE ARE
THREE TO GET YOU STARTED.

MILK (2008)

WATER (1985)

BEETLEJUICE (1988)

60

GOOD REASONS TO DO
DRY JANUARY #3

AFTER A FORTNIGHT YOU WILL
START TO FEEL THAT WARM GLOW
THAT ONLY THE TRULY SMUG AND
CONDESCENDING KNOW.

(61)

PUT ADMONISHING POST-IT NOTES AROUND THE HOUSE.

DON'T YOU DARE OPEN THIS BOTTLE!

WHERE'S YOUR WILLPOWER?

STOP BEING SO PATHETIC AND GO AND HAVE A RUN!

62

REMEMBER THE DANGERS
OF JUST ONE DRINK:

"SUBLIME IS
SOMETHING
YOU CHOKE
ON AFTER
A SHOT OF
TEQUILA."

(MARK Z. DANIELEWSKI)

63

TAKE IT ONE HOUR AT A TIME:
IF YOU GET A REAL HANKERING
FOR A DRINK, DON'T JUST SIT
THERE SUFFERING, GET UP OR
GO OUT AND DO SOMETHING
FOR 60 MINUTES – CLEAN THE
BATHROOM, GO FOR A WALK
– AND BY THE TIME YOU'VE
FINISHED THE URGE
WILL HAVE PASSED.

64

TAKE UP SOMETHING NEW.
WHAT ABOUT A SEWING BEE?
AFTER ALL YOU'RE GOING TO NEED
A LOT OF BUNTING FOR THAT END-
OF-CHALLENGE CELEBRATION ON
1 FEBRUARY (SEE TIP 13). JUST DON'T
JOIN A RUGBY CLUB, A CHOIR OR
A BRASS BAND — ALL PACKED
WITH PRODIGIOUS IMBIBERS.

(65)

PRACTISE

MIND OVER MATTER:
DRINK SQUASH IN A

PINT GLASS,

COKE IN A

WINE GLASS

AND BITTER LEMON IN A

WHISKY TUMBLER,

AND USE YOUR

IMAGINATION.

YOU REALLY DON'T NEED TO
DRINK TO ENJOY YOURSELF.
AS E.E. CUMMINGS WROTE:

**"HIS LIPS DRINK WATER BUT
HIS HEART DRINKS WINE."**

AND NANCY ASTOR CONCURRED:

**"ONE REASON I DON'T DRINK IS
THAT I WANT TO KNOW WHEN
I AM HAVING A GOOD TIME."**

67

AS IT HAS OFTEN BEEN SAID:

" **DRY JANUARY –** HOW TO MAKE THE MOST **DEPRESSING** MONTH OF THE YEAR **EVEN WORSE ...** "

– NOBODY EVER SAID IT WAS GOING TO BE EASY!

68

REMEMBER THAT CHRISTMAS
PUDDING THAT NO ONE REALLY
WANTED? MOST OF IT IS STILL AT
THE BACK OF THE FRIDGE WAITING
TO BE THROWN OUT AT EASTER.
BEFORE IT WAS PUT THERE, IT WAS
DROWNED IN BRANDY . . .
GO ON, DIG IT OUT AND INDULGE.

69

HAVE A LIST
OF DAILY TREATS
(MAYBE A PACKET
OF CRISPS OR A BAR
OF CHOCOLATE), WEEKLY
TREATS (A NIGHT AT THE
CINEMA), AND A BIG TREAT
FOR THE END OF THE MONTH
IF . . . NO, *WHEN!* . . . YOU MAKE IT
(A WEEKEND AWAY).

IF YOU HATE WASTE, AND SOMEONE HAS OPENED A BOTTLE OF WINE AND THE LAST GLASS IS JUST SITTING IN THERE LOOKING AT YOU, GRAB AN EMPTY ICE-CUBE TRAY, FILL IT WITH THE LEFTOVER WINE AND POP IT IN THE FREEZER: PERFECT ICE CUBES FOR FEBRUARY OR INSTANT GRAVY ENHANCERS.

PRACTICAL

71

SO, STEPHANIE, WHAT DO I DO IF
I'VE GIVEN UP ALONG WITH MY
PARTNER AND HE/SHE THEN GIVES
UP GIVING UP? WELL, READER,
IT'S CLEARLY NOT UNREASONABLE
IN THESE CIRCUMSTANCES TO
THREATEN DIVORCE, OR AT LEAST
MAKE THEM MOVE OUT UNTIL
1 FEBRUARY. ON THE PLUS SIDE,
THEY WILL NOW OWE YOU BIG
TIME. YOU HAVE THE MORAL HIGH
GROUND – USE IT WISELY!

72

IF YOU HAVE TO GO TO A PUB,
OPT OUT OF ROUNDS – THE
THOUGHT OF PAYING FOR
EVERYONE ELSE'S G&Ts AND
PINTS WHILE YOU'RE SIPPING AN
ORANGE JUICE WILL DRIVE YOU
INSANE. INSTEAD, SIT THEM OUT,
ASK THE BARMAN POLITELY FOR
TAP WATER (WHICH THEY *HAVE*
TO SERVE YOU WITH) AND WATCH
YOUR BANK BALANCE MOUNT UP.

73

DOG-WALKING IS A GREAT
WAY TO GET OUT OF THE HOUSE
INSTEAD OF SETTLING DOWN
WITH A G&T. IF YOU HAVEN'T GOT
ONE, ADOPT ONE. REMEMBER,
A DOG IS FOR DRY JANUARY,
NOT JUST FOR CHRISTMAS.

74

IT'S TRADITIONAL TO WET THE
BABY'S HEAD, SO YOU'LL NEED TO
STAY STRONG WHEN ALL AROUND
YOU ARE CLINKING GLASSES.
BABIES MAY BE CUTE BUT THEN
AGAIN, THINK OF THE ENDLESS
NAPPY CHANGING AND THE LACK
OF SLEEP. A LOT OF BABIES ARE
MADE WHILE INTOXICATED (THE
PARENTS, OBVIOUSLY, NOT THE
BABIES). DO YOURSELF A FAVOUR,
AND STICK TO LEMONADE.

(75)

IF YOU GO TRAVELLING
AROUND THE UK IN

JANUARY,

MAKE SURE YOU GIVE THE
FOLLOWING PLACES A MISS:

BEER IN DEVON,

BRANDISTON IN NORFOLK,

WINESTEAD

IN YORKSHIRE AND, IN
TIPSY OLD SCOTLAND,
LAGA, SIADAR AND THE

ISLE OF RUM!

TO MAKE SURE YOU DON'T
GET INVITED TO ANY BOOZY
BURNS NIGHT CELEBRATIONS ON
25 JANUARY, PUT THIS QUOTE BY
CHARLES LAMB AS YOUR
FACEBOOK STATUS:

"I HAVE BEEN TRYING ALL MY
LIFE TO LIKE SCOTSMEN, AND AM
OBLIGED TO DESIST FROM
THE EXPERIMENT IN DESPAIR."

(77)

*ONLY READ THIS TIP IF YOU NORMALLY
HAVE FOUR DRINKS PER DAY OR MORE!*

APPARENTLY, SOME SCIENTISTS
RECKON ONE DRINK A DAY *ADDS*
30 MINUTES TO YOUR LIFE SPAN –
BUT EVERY DRINK AFTER THE FIRST
REDUCES IT BY 15 MINUTES. SO IF
YOU'RE A FOUR-A-DAY PERSON,
AFTER DRY JANUARY YOU'LL HAVE
7¾ HOURS TO PLAY WITH IN
FEBRUARY ... WHICH OF COURSE
YOU'LL PROBABLY SPEND IN THE PUB.

PUT THESE LINES ON THE OUTSIDE OF YOUR DRINKS CABINET:

ONE EVENING IN OCTOBER,

WHEN I WAS ONE-FIFTH SOBER

AND TAKING HOME A LOAD WITH MANLY PRIDE,

MY POOR FEET BEGAN TO STUTTER,

SO I LAY DOWN IN THE GUTTER

AND A PIG CAME UP AND LAY DOWN BY MY SIDE.

THEN WE SANG 'IT'S ALL FAIR WEATHER'

AND 'GOOD FELLOWS GET TOGETHER'

TILL A LADY PASSING BY WAS HEARD TO SAY,

'YOU CAN TELL A MAN WHO BOOZES

BY THE COMPANY HE CHOOSES,'

AND THE PIG GOT UP AND SLOWLY WALKED AWAY.

79

" **WHEN I READ**
ABOUT THE EVILS OF
DRINKING,
I GAVE UP
READING. "

(HENRY WISEMAN)

DON'T GIVE UP READING
THIS BOOK THOUGH –
WE CAN DO THIS!

80

GOOD REASONS TO DO
DRY JANUARY #4

YOUR COMPLEXION WILL
START TO IMPROVE; YOU'LL
START TO SLEEP BETTER;
AND YOUR CHOLESTEROL
LEVELS WILL GO DOWN.

DID YOU KNOW YOU CAN
BUY ALCOHOL-SCENTED
CANDLES ONLINE?
LIGHT A RUM-FLAVOURED
ONE UP, POUR YOURSELF
A TUMBLER OF COKE AND
LET YOUR BRAIN
DO THE REST.

82

IF NOTHING BUT THE AWFUL BRAIN-DECIMATING CLANG OF A HANGOVER WILL KEEP YOU OFF THE BOOZE, WHY NOT REPLICATE ITS EFFECTS BY PUTTING ON A BLACK SABBATH/TCHAIKOVSKY/ MUSE CD AT FULL VOLUME AND STANDING NEXT TO THE LOUDSPEAKER WHILE EATING A LARGE BOWL OF ICE CREAM AND STARING INTENTLY AT YOUR COMPUTER SCREEN FOR AN HOUR OR SO BEFORE BEDTIME.

TOUGH

LOVE

83

AVOID ALL THINGS THAT MAKE
YOU FEEL YOU NEED A DRINK:
IT'S A GREAT EXCUSE TO STOP
PHONING YOUR MOTHER.

(84)

IF YOUR FRIENDS ARE
MAKING FUN
OF YOUR DESIGNATED DRIVER STATUS,
GET YOUR OWN BACK BY
DROPPING THEM OFF AT THE

WRONG
HOUSE.

ONE DRINK ISN'T THE END
OF THE WORLD. IF YOU HAVE
A MOMENT OF WEAKNESS,
PUT IT BEHIND YOU AND
KEEP GOING.

86

VOLUNTEER AT A HOMELESS
SHELTER FOR A FEW NIGHTS
IN JANUARY – YOU'LL DO SOME
GOOD, BE OUT OF THE WAY OF ANY
INTOXICANTS FOR A FEW HOURS,
AND IT WILL MAKE YOU COUNT
YOUR BLESSINGS.

87

IF YOU FANCY YOURSELF AS
A GREAT LOVER, REMEMBER
WHAT SHAKESPEARE HAD TO
SAY ABOUT ALCOHOL:

"IT PROVOKES THE

DESIRE

BUT IT TAKES AWAY THE

PERFORMANCE."

(MACBETH, ACT II, SCENE III)

IF YOU'RE INVITED TO A FUNCTION WHERE ALCOHOL WILL BE SERVED, THEN DRIVE — EVEN IF IT'S JUST DOWN THE ROAD. FORGET ABOUT SAVING THE PLANET FOR A MONTH, AND CONCENTRATE ON SAVING YOUR LIVER.

89

A CHEAT'S TIP:

LIQUEUR CHOCOLATES DON'T COUNT – GREAT FOR MOMENTS OF WEAKNESS.

90

IF YOU'RE SHORT OF
SUPPORT FROM FRIENDS AND
RELATIVES, TRY WEBSITES LIKE
JOINCLUBSODA.CO.UK, AN ONLINE
SUPPORT GROUP PACKED WITH
HELPFUL IDEAS AND OFFERS.

PRACTICAL

91

MAKE A LIST OF THE MOST CRINGE-INDUCING THINGS YOU'VE EVER DONE WHILE UNDER THE INFLUENCE AND REFER TO IT WHENEVER YOU FEEL TEMPTED. HERE ARE MY THREE TO START YOU OFF, IN INCREASING ORDER OF EMBARRASSMENT.

1 THREW UP OVER MY MOTHER-IN-LAW'S YORKSHIRE TERRIER.

2 PROPOSED TO AN ICELANDIC BACKPACKER I'D MET HALF AN HOUR BEFORE.

3 BOUGHT A *BLAKE'S 7* DVD FROM AMAZON.

92

BOOK A
WEEK'S HOLIDAY IN
IRAN
STARTING ON
24 JANUARY.

93

"FIRST YOU TAKE A DRINK, THEN THE DRINK TAKES A DRINK, THEN THE DRINK TAKES YOU."

(F. SCOTT FITZGERALD)

TRIGGER POINTS #3
FUNERALS

THIS IS A TRICKY ONE. IS IT
DISRESPECTFUL NOT TO DRINK
TO THE RECENTLY DEPARTED?
IF YOU ARE PRESSED, USE THE OLD
ANTIBIOTIC EXCUSE (SEE TIP 29).

(95)

DRY JANUARY
IS A GREAT OPPORTUNITY TO
DE-CLUTTER
YOUR LIFE AND TO
MAKE TIME
FOR THE PEOPLE WHO REALLY
MATTER TO YOU. MAKE A LIST OF
'FRIENDS'
WHOSE COMPANY YOU CAN ONLY
STAND IF YOU ARE DRINKING
AND STRIKE THEM FROM YOUR
CONTACT LISTS.

EVERY TIME YOU FEEL LIKE A
DRINK, GO FOR A WALK ROUND
THE BLOCK, REPEATING THE
FOLLOWING VERSE.

THERE WAS A YOUNG WOMAN CALLED MARY,
WHOSE ALCOHOL BILL WAS QUITE SCARY,
SO SHE SCREWED UP HER NERVE,
GAVE THE WINE BARS A SWERVE,
AND SIGNED UP FOR DRY JANUARY.

97

AFTER THE FIRST GLASS, YOU SEE THINGS AS YOU WISH THEY WERE. AFTER THE SECOND, YOU SEE THINGS AS THEY ARE NOT. FINALLY, YOU SEE THINGS AS THEY REALLY ARE, AND THAT IS THE MOST HORRIBLE THING IN THE WORLD.

(OSCAR WILDE)

THE GREAT IRISH PLAYWRIGHT REMINDING US THAT SOBRIETY IS MORE HAPPILY DELUSIONAL THAN DRUNKENNESS.

98

IF YOU'RE STRUGGLING
TOWARDS THE END OF THE MONTH,
WHY NOT AVAIL YOURSELF OF THE
GROWING NUMBER OF COMPANIES
WHO, FOR A PRICE, WILL KIDNAP
YOU? JUST TELL THEM YOU WANT
TO BE DENIED ALCOHOL AND
RELEASED ON 1 FEBRUARY.

DESPERATE

MEASURES

99

IF YOU'RE FEELING DOWN, PUT ON YOUR FAVOURITE COMEDY DVD – ALCOHOL IS A DEPRESSANT AND WILL ONLY MAKE YOU FEEL MORE MAUDLIN. AS PITTACUS LORE (NO, ME NEITHER) SAID:

"IF YOU EVER KNOW A MAN WHO TRIES TO DROWN HIS SORROWS, KINDLY INFORM HIM HIS SORROWS KNOW HOW **TO SWIM.**"

100

DON'T BRAG ABOUT YOUR CLEAN
STATUS – NO ONE LIKES A VIRTUOUS
VIRGINIA OR VERNON, AND PEOPLE
WILL TAKE GREAT DELIGHT IN
PLACING EXTRA TEMPTATION IN
YOUR WAY AND TRIPPING YOU UP
JUST WHEN YOU THINK YOU'RE HOME
AND DRY. THREE THINGS NOT TO
SAY DURING DRY JANUARY:

1 'IT'S A LOT EASIER THAN I
THOUGHT IT WOULD BE.'

2 'I THINK I MIGHT CARRY ON
UNTIL EASTER.'

3 'YOU SHOULD TRY IT – IT WOULD DO
WONDERS FOR YOUR SKIN.'

101

AS THE END
OF THE MONTH
APPROACHES,
USE THE MONEY
YOU'VE SAVED TO
BOOK A FEW DAYS
AT A SPA TO SEE YOU
TO THE FINISH LINE.

WHILE YOU ARE
INDULGING YOURSELF,
THINK ABOUT
ALL THE HEALTH
BENEFITS YOU
HAVE GAINED
THROUGH YOUR
31 DRY DAYS.

YOU DID IT!

Well . . . how did it go? Did you do it? Did you nearly do it, with one or two lapses? Or did you crash and burn at the first hurdle in a horrible, hair-of-the-dog car-wreck of a Dry January?

If you made it, congratulations, you must be feeling very pleased with yourself. Just don't go on too much of a celebratory bender, or you'll undo all your good work.

And if you came up short, well, never mind — you deserve a big pat on the back for trying. And all is not lost — why not treat this as a dry run for Sober October? Whatever you do, you can console yourself that you almost certainly got further than me!

CHEERS!